GROWING UP WITH MONSTERS:
MY TIMES AT UNIVERSAL
STUDIOS, IN RHYMES!

Growing Up With Monsters: My Times at Universal Studios, in Rhymes!

by Carla Laemmle and
Daniel Kinske, LCDR, U.S.N.

Foreword by Ray Bradbury

Illustrated by Jack Davis and Hermann Mejia

BearManor Media
2009

Growing Up With Monsters:
My Times at Universal Studios, in Rhymes!

© 2009 Carla Laemmle and Daniel Kinske

Illustrations by Jack Davis and Hermann Mejia

For information, address:

BearManor Media
P. O. Box 71426
Albany, GA 31708

bearmanormedia.com

Cover art by Jack Davis

Cover layout by John Teehan

Typesetting and layout by John Teehan

Published in the USA by BearManor Media

ISBN—1-59393-341-X

We dedicate this book and story,
to the memory of our friend Forrey.

Forrest J. Ackerman 1916~2009

This book is for every person in the world who cares about *The Hunchback of Notre Dame*, *The Phantom of the Opera*, and all the great horror films of all time. It mustn't be missed.

–Ray Bradbury

Boo!

The tale I'm about to tell is true!

These vampires, werewolves, and witches,

are still apt to keep you all in stitches...

My neighborhood teamed with fantastic creatures,

from now classic Universal film features.

ONCE UPON A TIME, five score years ago,
I was born in the windy city of Chicago.
That was in the great state of Illinois—
My parents didn't care if I was a girl or a boy.
On October 20th, I was born fit and fine,
That grand old year was 1909!

MY FIRST FRIEND was not a monster or scary,

"Philbin" was her last name, but I called her Mary.

My father asked his brother Carl to visit our fair city,

he did, saw Mary, and thought her oh so pretty.

He owned Universal Studios in California out
    West,

and invited Mary there to perform a motion picture
    test.

She did very well on that audition,

and her dreams came to fruition.

Now her-story,

is his-story!

LESS THAN A YEAR LATER in nineteen twenty-one,
Carl wrote my dad a letter that was fun.
It invited us all, if we thought we could—
to live in the magical land of Hollywood!
With open arms and generosity he did jot,
for us to reside on his Universal Studios lot!

SO MY MOM, DAD, GRANDMA AND I left during a day
of rain,
and thankfully made it safely aboard a West bound
train.
I saw everything going by and by,
passing over tie after tie.

4

A MAN FROM UNIVERSAL met us all at the station,

and drove us to our new studio city destination.

Our household goods were back in Chicago,

Our comfort we thought we'd have to forego.

But instead of arriving to a cold and empty
    apartment,

It was fully-furnished—courtesy of the property
    department!

MY UNCLE BOUGHT that land of cinematic charm,
when it was nothing but a remote chicken farm.
For films he used some animals and added a zoo,
with horses, elephants, lions, and tigers too!
My favorites were an elusive camel named "Houdini",
and "Jiggs," the resident chimpanzee.

MY FATHER WORKED ON THE LOT, but in his down time,
entertained his director friend—Erich von Stroheim.
He was a man America "loved to hate,"
but to dad he was a chess partner—"check mate!"
I tested with him for a part in "The Merry Widow",
being too young, that part went right out the
    window...

MY MOM HAD a certain preoccupation,

that in addition to roles, I attain a proper education.

She found a tutor who taught at the Hollywood
Hotel—

it looked kind of haunted, but all and all was quite
swell.

The ceiling had painted stars, each with an actor's
name,

that was the beginning of today's Hollywood Walk
of Fame!

LONG BEFORE SOUND technologically was around,
there were more hands-on studio tours to be found.
Many of the people that I saw and often met,
could get very close to most any filming set.
As a Laemmle I had a pass to roam the lot freely,
It was an entertaining pastime I did quite frequently.
I remember one day I was especially glad I came,
witnessing a scene from *The Hunchback of Notre
    Dame!*

QUASIMODO'S CHARACTER lacked certain social
  graces—
played by Lon Chaney, Sr.—the "man of 1,000
  faces."
Though lots of time it would take up.
he always did his own make-up.
He had a hunch on his back,
and his teeth were all black.
He inserted walnuts in his mouth for weeks,
which was done to puff out his cheeks.
Not one to put up facades or fronts,
he invariably performed all his own stunts.
Watching this great actor was certainly a sight
  to see,
that was way back in nineteen twenty-three!

A PLACE WAS PROVIDED for the actors to meet—
to rest, to talk, to greet, and to eat.
It had everything from steak to dairy,
And was called the Universal Studio Commissary.
No matter what the time of day or mood,
There were always monsters having their food.
To me it was always a fun sight to see—
even if the stars were just having their tea.

THOUGH SILENT AND CAPTURED in picturesque
pantomimes,
The Phantom of the Opera played the organ
chimes.
A climactic scene where Mary actually did fret,
was filmed on a secluded closed set.
My friend Mary's most difficult cinematic tasking,
was the frightful scene of the Phantom's unmasking.

I WAS THE PRIMA BALLERINA in my dancing scene,
back in 1925 when I was only sixteen.
I enjoyed pirouetting, but did so without a sound,
twirling about while the Phantom lurked around!

ONE DAY as an extra I proudly found,
That I had the first line of horror film sound.
I simply read them loud, true, and sure—
from my Transylvanian travel brochure.
This has always been a fond recollection,
in a film where Bela Lugosi had no reflection!

THIS "BIT" PART IN DRACULA was in a coach,
with Mr. Renfield, who chomped on a roach.
His real life name was Dwight Frye—
really that gentle soul wouldn't hurt a fly.
He caught me in the scene with the pamphlet I read,
and saved me from hitting and hurting my head!
This film did not end his horror genre blitz—
In *Frankenstein* he played the equally crazy Fritz.

EVENTUALLY UNIVERSAL'S horror films of fright,
turned to a kind of funny and comedic delight.
Soon every mumbling monster said, "Hello,"
to the bumbling comedians, Abbott and Costello!
They had something the audiences took after,
backed up by box office success and laughter.
The Mummy, Dracula, and Wolfman paired no more,
not until *Van Helsing* in 2004!

IN ALL THIS UNIVERSAL studio horror history,

you might ask, what would become of me?

I met a man named Ray whom I started to date,

Forty-two years of happiness was our eventual
     fate!

We traveled to Baja where he always helped bait
     my hook,

while I helped him with his best-selling *Sea of
     Cortez* book

After meeting him, I never wanted to find another,

Like the Frankenstein's bride, we were *made* for
     each other!

SO THESE MONSTERS in which I did grow up,

were just studio actors in elaborate make-up.

I saw them from the beginning when filming was silent,

These days, it's technology upon which we're so
    reliant.

These horror films are classics year after year,

that they might be forgotten is my **UNIVERSAL FEAR!**

Above: My toes were telling me something— harbingers of my happy feet future. November 1909.

Left: Before the Roaring Twenties happened, I was enjoying the Dancing Tens in Chicago.

Above: Playing in my new front yard in Universal Studios. Our house to the right and the back of the Old New York Street set adjacent to it. My dog Dixie and I are just having fun. Circa 1921.

Bottom left: My father, Joseph, on the left, and his director friend, Erich Von Stroheim on the right, on the set of *Foolish Wives* in 1922.

Bottom right: Extremely rare stone-lithograph one-sheet (27x41") movie poster for the 1923 film, which I saw being filmed at age thirteen. Courtesy of the Ron Borst Collection.

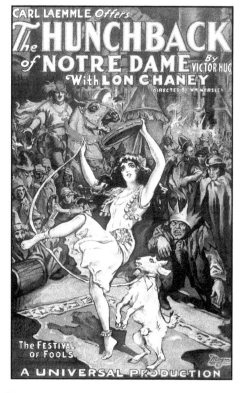

Left: I'm seated next to my childhood friend, Mary Philbin, in 1924 at my 15th birthday party. How fun to be in a film with her the following year!" Paul Kohner, seated in the bottom right-hand corner would later marry my fellow *Dracula* alumni, albeit the Spanish version, Lupita Tovar.

Right: Reuniting with Mary sixty-four years later in 1988 at her home in Hollywood.

Left: Artist interpretation of the Phantom atop the Paris Opera House in one of eight poster variants for this film—only two of which feature the Phantom. Universal 1925.

Top Left: The second poster showing the Phantom, and arguably the only one that actually depicts Lon Chaney, Sr. in the role. Sold at Heritage Galleries in Dallas, Texas in November 2008 for $155,350.00."

Top right: Poster (14"x36")."

Left: "Window card (14x22)"

Top: Title card (11"x14") shows Lon Chaney, Sr. sans make-up.

Bottom: Where's Carla? Can you find me as the *Prima Ballerina* on the opulent Paris Opera House set in the *Phantom of the Opera*?

Right: Here's a close-up of me with my hands over my head and doing a little dance—or a *Danse Macabre?*

Above: All of the ballerinas freshly in our costumes for the days shoot in early 1925. The film was released in Hollywood three days before my sixteenth birthday on October 17th, 1925.

Left: Here's a close-up of my ballerina costume. It differed from the others and was more ornate, but not because I was a Prima Dona, but because I was the Prima Ballerina!

22

Top left: Visiting the Paris Opera House set over eighty-years later with my co-author, Daniel, as the Phantom.

Top right: Daniel, and our young—but very tall, editor Seth, are presenting me with a very apropos 99th birthday present—a lovely little Lon!"

Right: My mother Belle and I, with Uncle Carl, at a Los Angles train station picking up a newly-arrived cousin 1927. It was only six years earlier, when my mother, father, grandmother, and I arrive from Chicago in 1921.

Left: Uncle Carl and I when I played "Sally" at the Shrine Light Opera in 1928.

Right: Mary and Conrad Veidt in a melodrama horror film that you can't help smiling too—well, maybe not—as Conrad's character, Gwynplaine, had a permanent carved smile, which was a surgeon's task, so he would have to laugh at the folly of his father who died in the Iron Mask. Filmed in 1927, but released in 1928

Left: A lobby card showing the hand-tined pictorial image of Mary and Conrad.

Right: The one-sheet, style "B", to *Dracula*. Universal, 1931.

Left: An artists interpretation of Bela Lugosi and Dwight Frye's characters in the style "F" version.

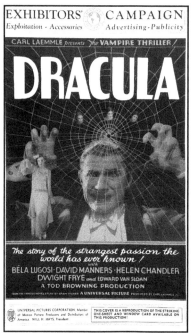

Above: This original press book to *Dracula* gives you an idea of how many poster versions (most non-extant now) were used to promote this very popular film, successfully adapted from the stage version.

Below: Being caught by Dwight Frye as Mr. Renfield in the Transylvanian coach, in 1931.

Above: One of only two scene cards known to exist from the Spanish version of *Dracula*, filmed on the same set, but at night—when we and the armadillos had gone to bed, but the bats were out in droves.

Below: Lupita Tovar, who played Eva in the Spanish version—equivalent to Helen Chandler's Mina Harker character in the English Language version. With a combined age of 198 years, we've given even the immortal Dracula a run for his money—and we are the only living cast members these near eighty year old films.

Left: The beautiful poster for *Frankenstein*, also released in 1931. There are only five known copies and when they are up for auction fetch higher and higher prices—$189,000 being a recent remittance, though in the future might seem a pitiful pittance.

Below: An original lobby card showing Dwight Frye as Fritz, harassing Boris Karloff as Frankenstein's monster—he elicited similar audience pity and pathos as did Lon Chaney's Quasimodo character—trapped in repulsive exteriors, but brimming with beautiful interiors.

Right: The only extant one-sheet from the 1932 classic—and it's a 'mirackle' this one even exists. Used on the cover of the imitable horror poster book *Graven Images* featuring the incomparable horror poster collection of Ron Borst.

Left: *The Mummy* one-sheet owned by Todd Feiertag, which sold in 1997 for over $453,000.00 still holds the highest price realized for a horror poster, but the Fritz Lang Science Fiction classic, *Metropolis* (UFA, 1927), sold in 2005 for $690,000.00 and is still the all-time highest priced movie poster of all time—you could buy a lot of popcorn for that amount!"

Left: Another Edgar Allen Poe inspired tale with two Universal Monster titans, it sold recently for over $286,000.00 at Heritage Galleries. Proving the prices continue to get more monstrous as there are so few posters this wondrous!

Right: One-sheet and half-sheets for the perennial James Whale sequel, which is one of the few ever done of ANY movie to be arguably better than the original film.

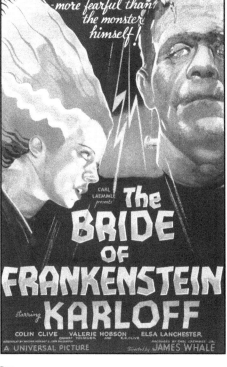

Above: "The Borst of Los Angeles" is the owner of this rare 1935 six-sheet—oversize classic horror posters are exceedingly rare.

Left: A one-sheet variant from the film.

Left: Another Poe-inspired poster with Karloff and Lugosi.

Below: Even the children of monsters did well as in these two classics.

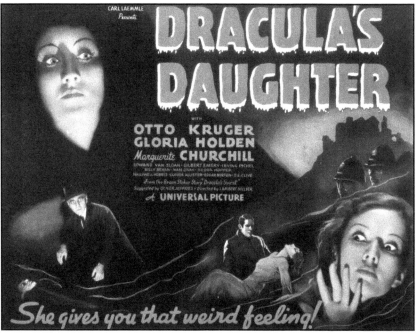

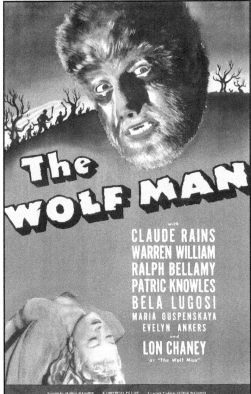

Left: London's Lycan takes a backseat to Lon Chaney, Jr's most memorable monster role. Claude Rains has a more visible role as his father in this first of many in the Wolf Man series.

Left: The monsters popularity and those of Abbott and Costello were both waning a bit in the late 40s, but when Universal put them together starting with this first in the popular "meeting monsters" series in 1948—they were both reanimated and rejuvenated.

Below: From *Dracula* to this denizen of the deep, Universal reigned supreme again as the horror king with this 1954 classic that spawned two sequels.

Above: Reminiscing with Ray Bradbury as he signs autographs for fans at Forrey Ackerman's 90th birthday party in 2006.

Left: The fact that I still get fan requests to sign *Phantom of the Opera* (and *Dracula*) memorabilia over eight and a half decades after the film was first released, is one reason I wanted to do this book!

Below: Even our Governor, and an actor who has dealt with his fair share of monstrous creatures, was happy to receive a signed *Phantom of the Opera* print from me. He enjoyed visiting Daniel and I so much, that we are pretty sure "he'll be back!"

In helping from all things from Dracula to Frank,

here are a few fine souls we'd like to thank:

Jack Davis, Sam Scali, Ray Bradbury, Alexandra Bradbury,
Seth Lemich Almberg, Ben Ohmart, Woolsey Ackerman,
Marc Wannamaker, Jeff Pirtle, Krista Bolling,
and Cindy Chang at Universal Studios.